Cha

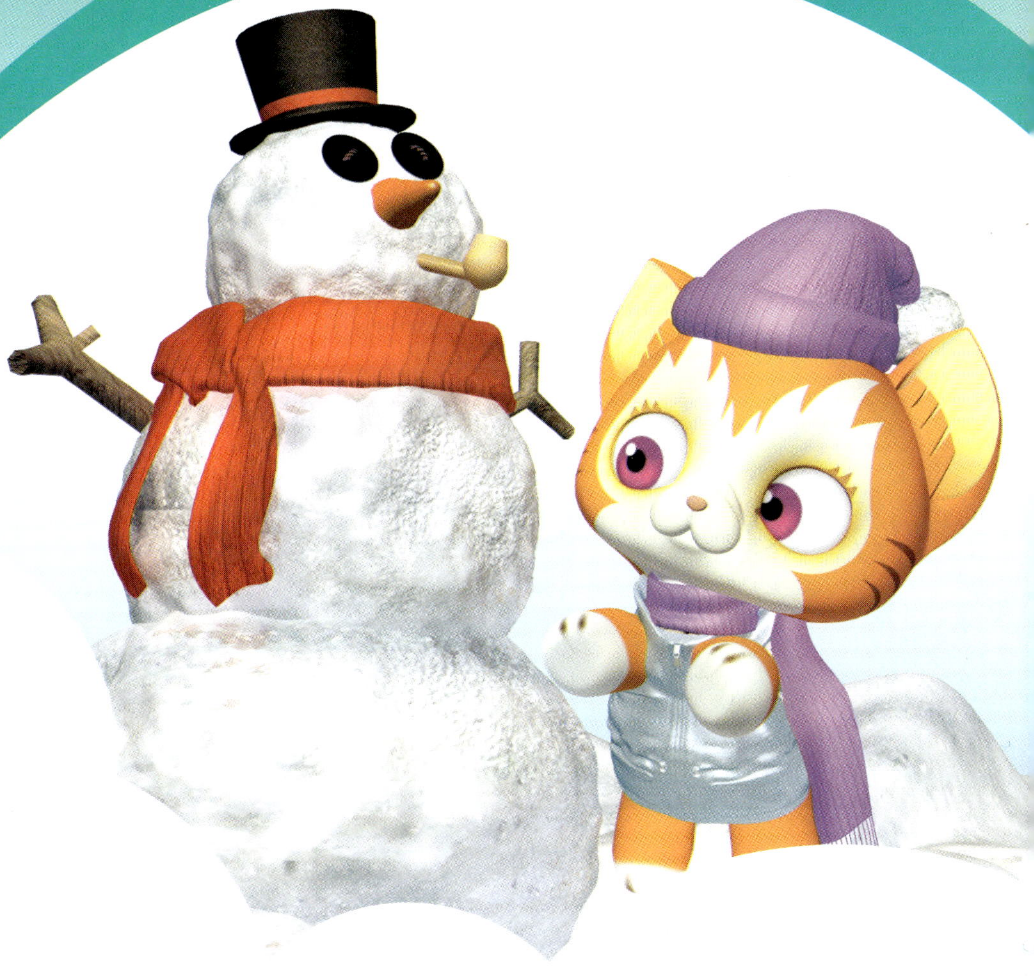

PEARSON

Glenview, Illinois • Boston, Massachusetts
Chandler, Arizona • Upper Saddle River, New Jersey

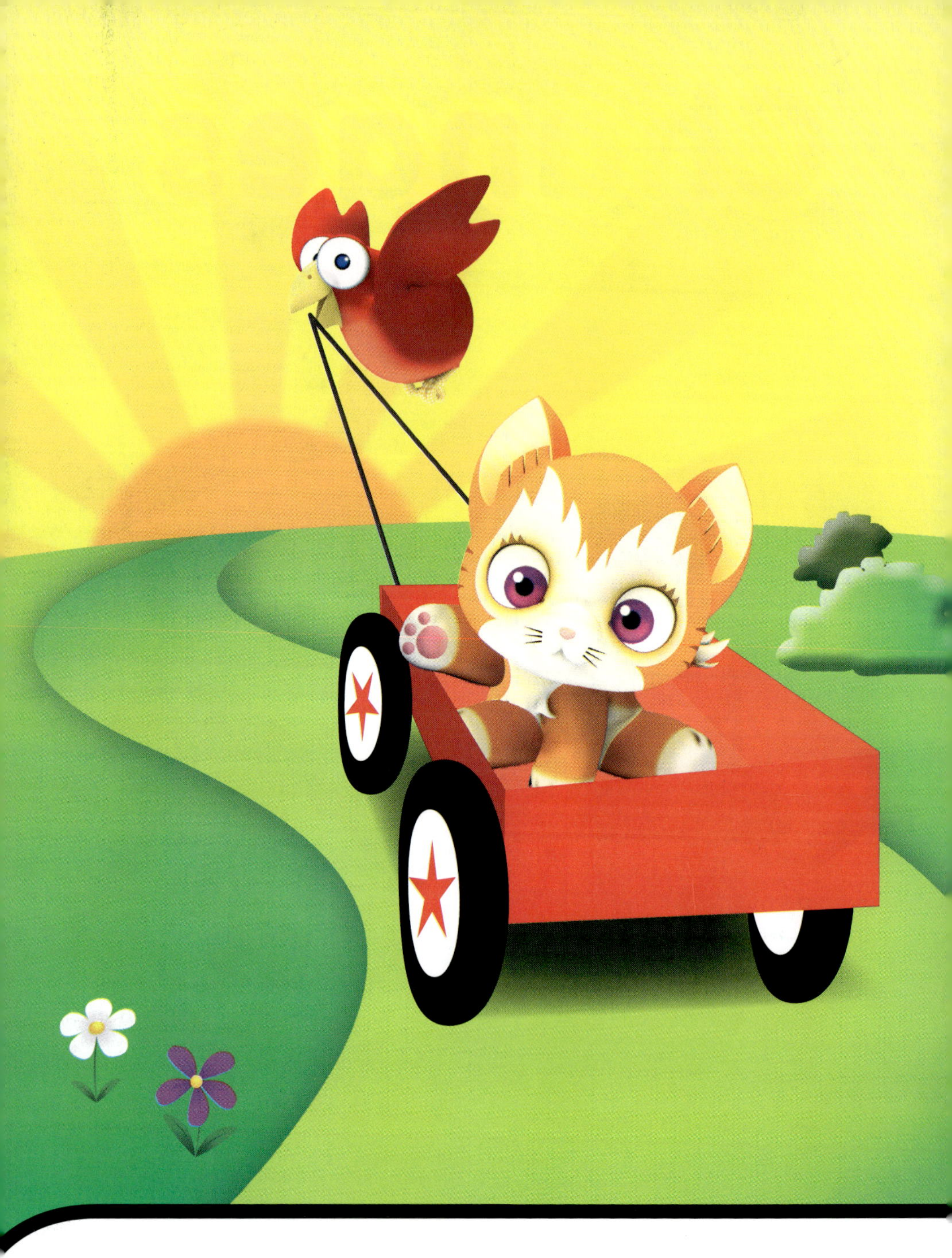

day

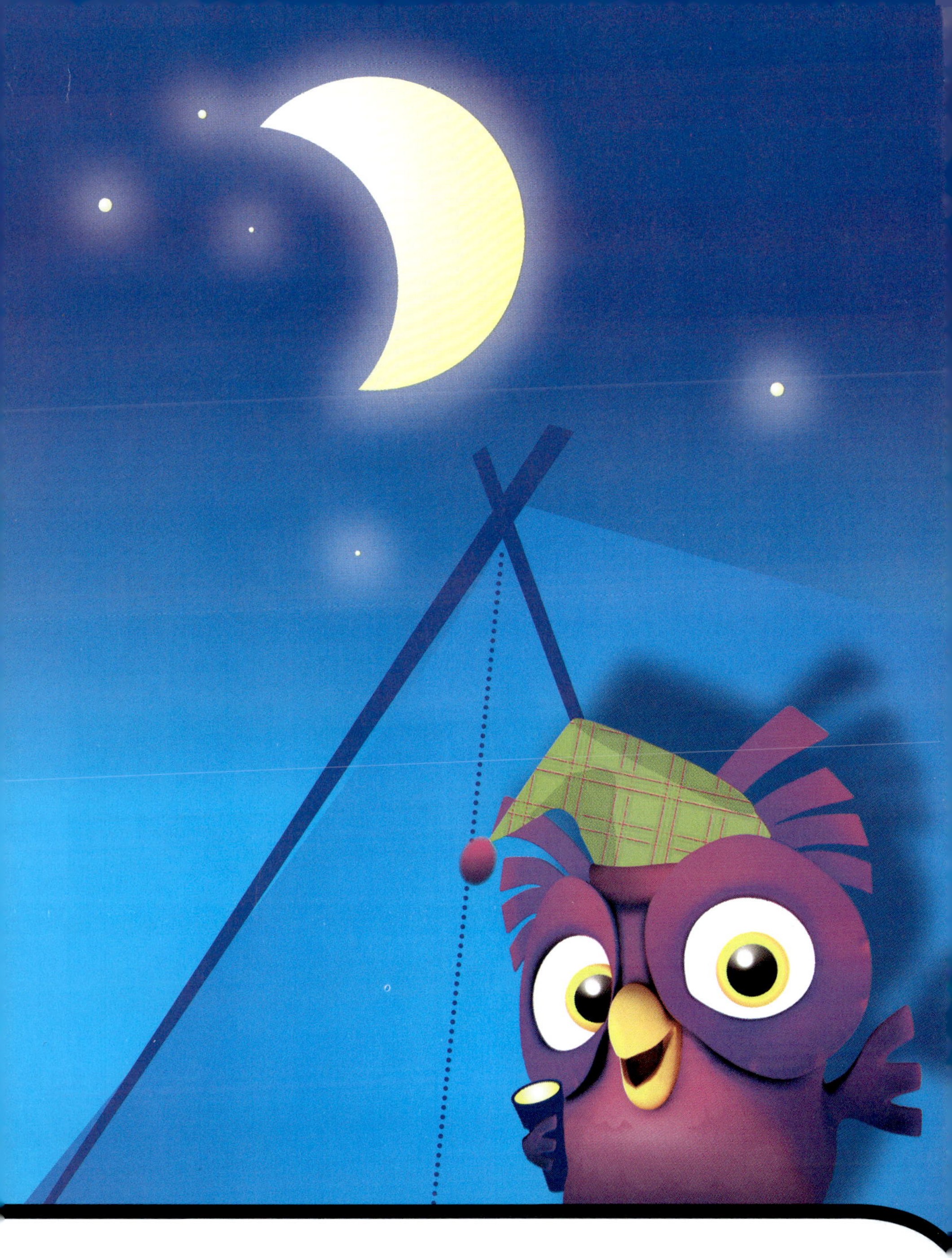

night

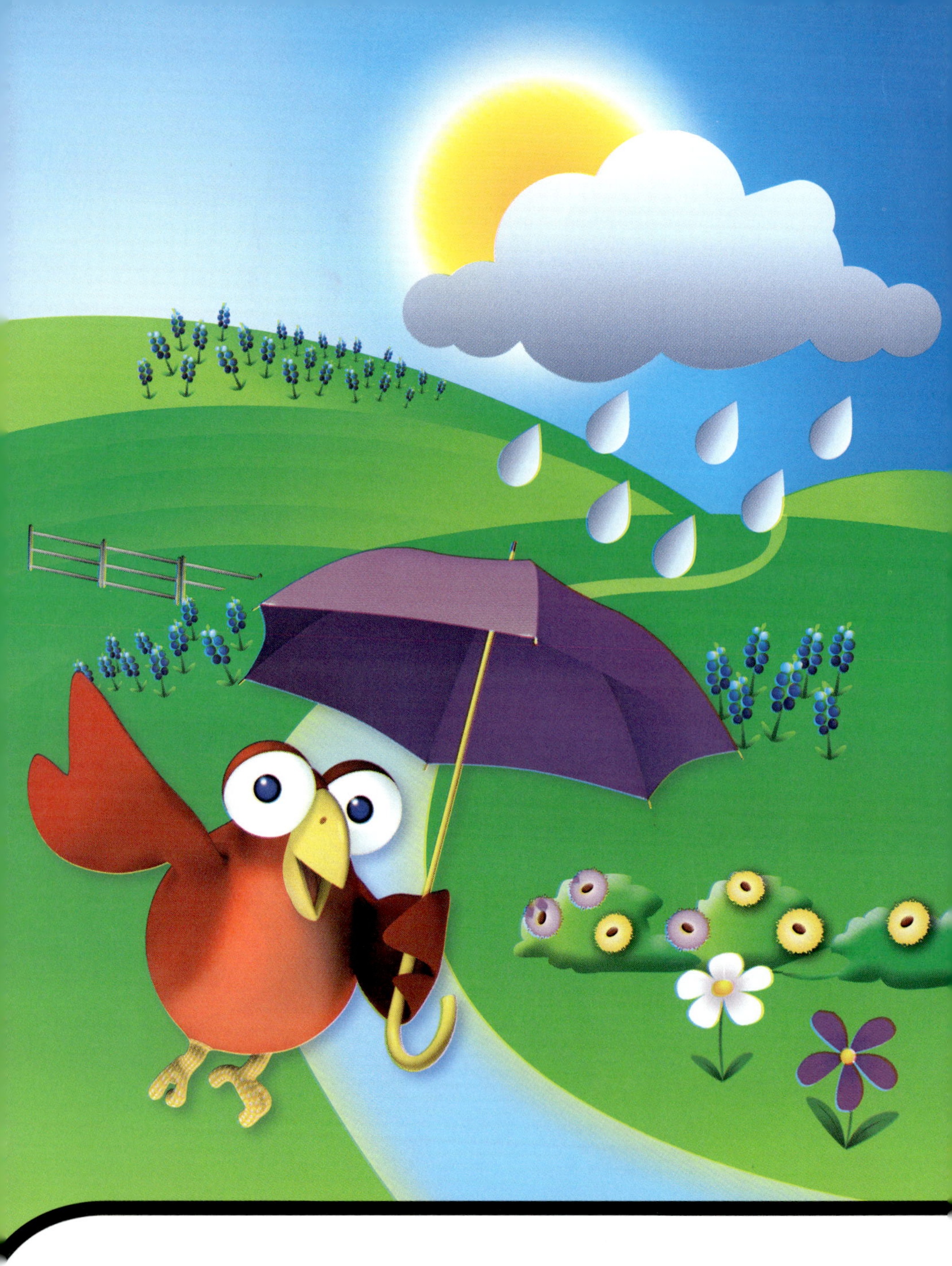

spring

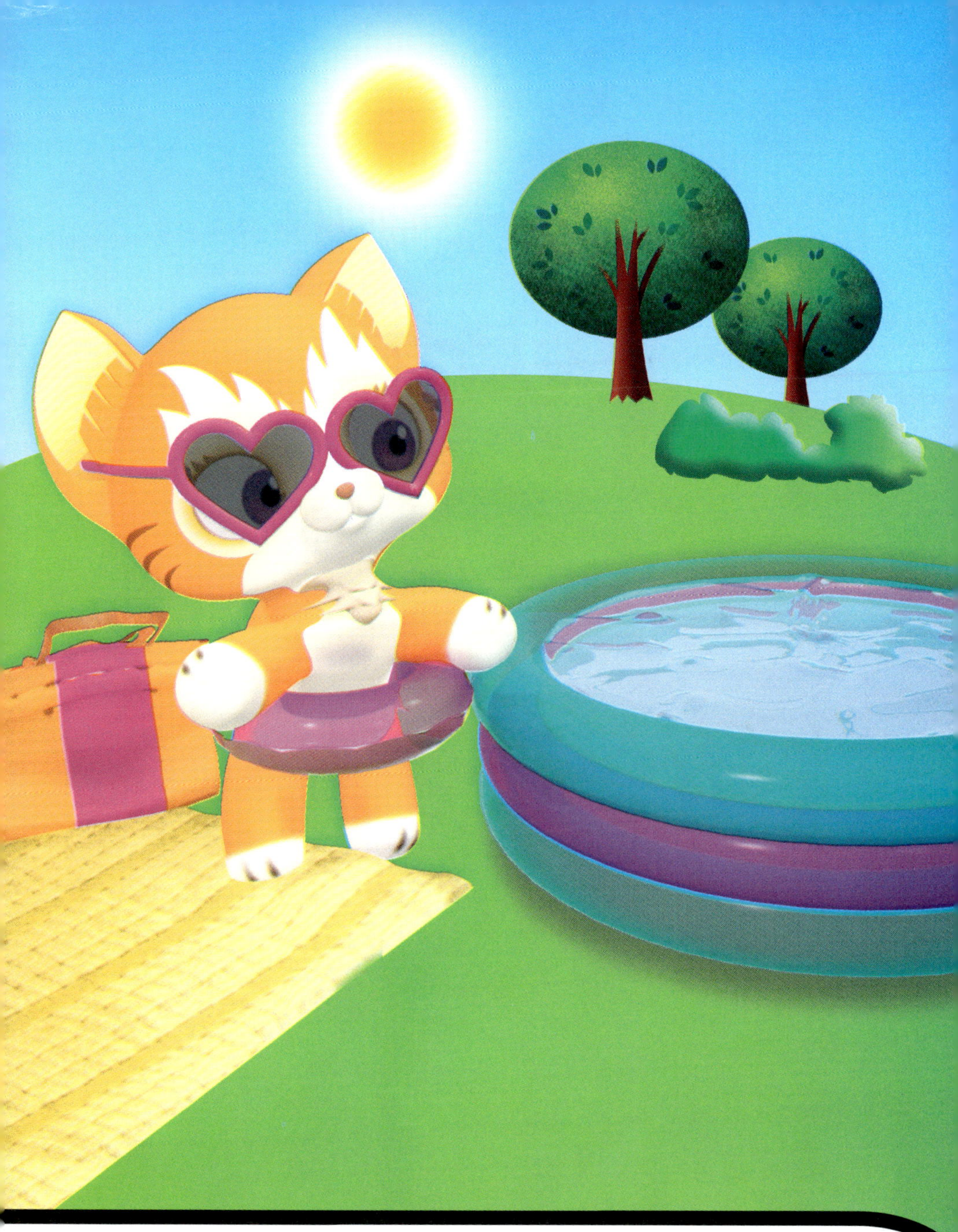

summer

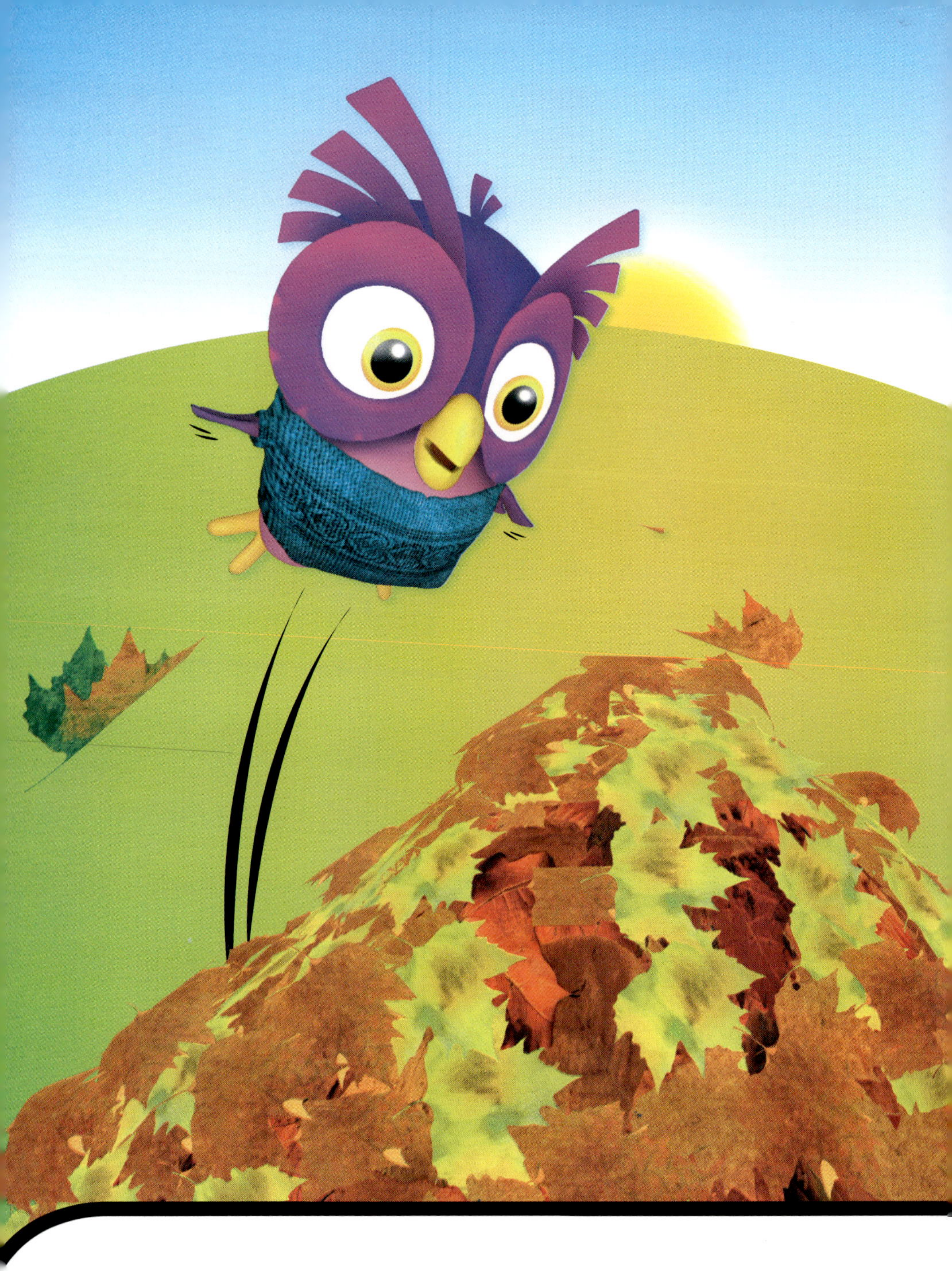

fall

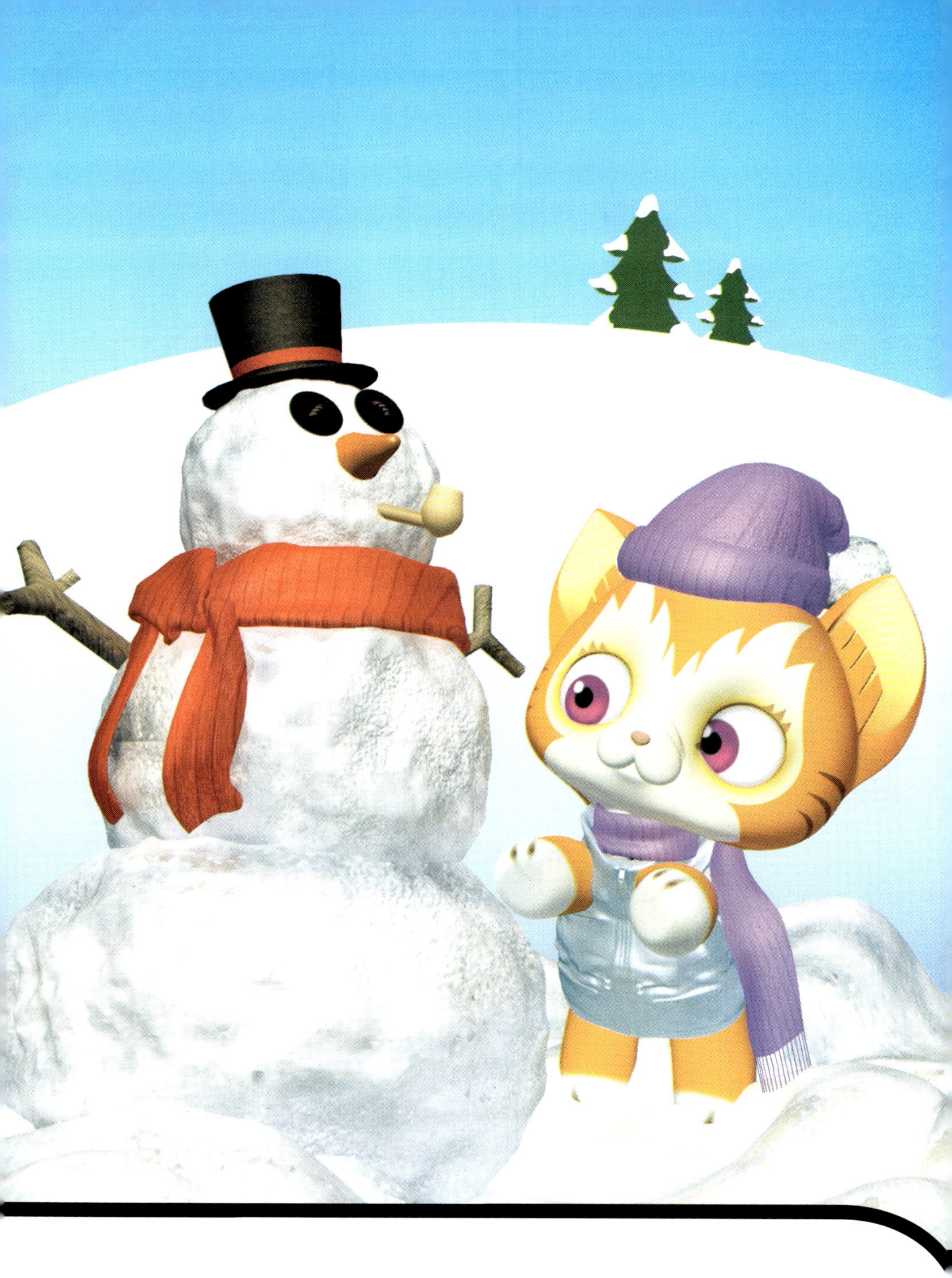

winter

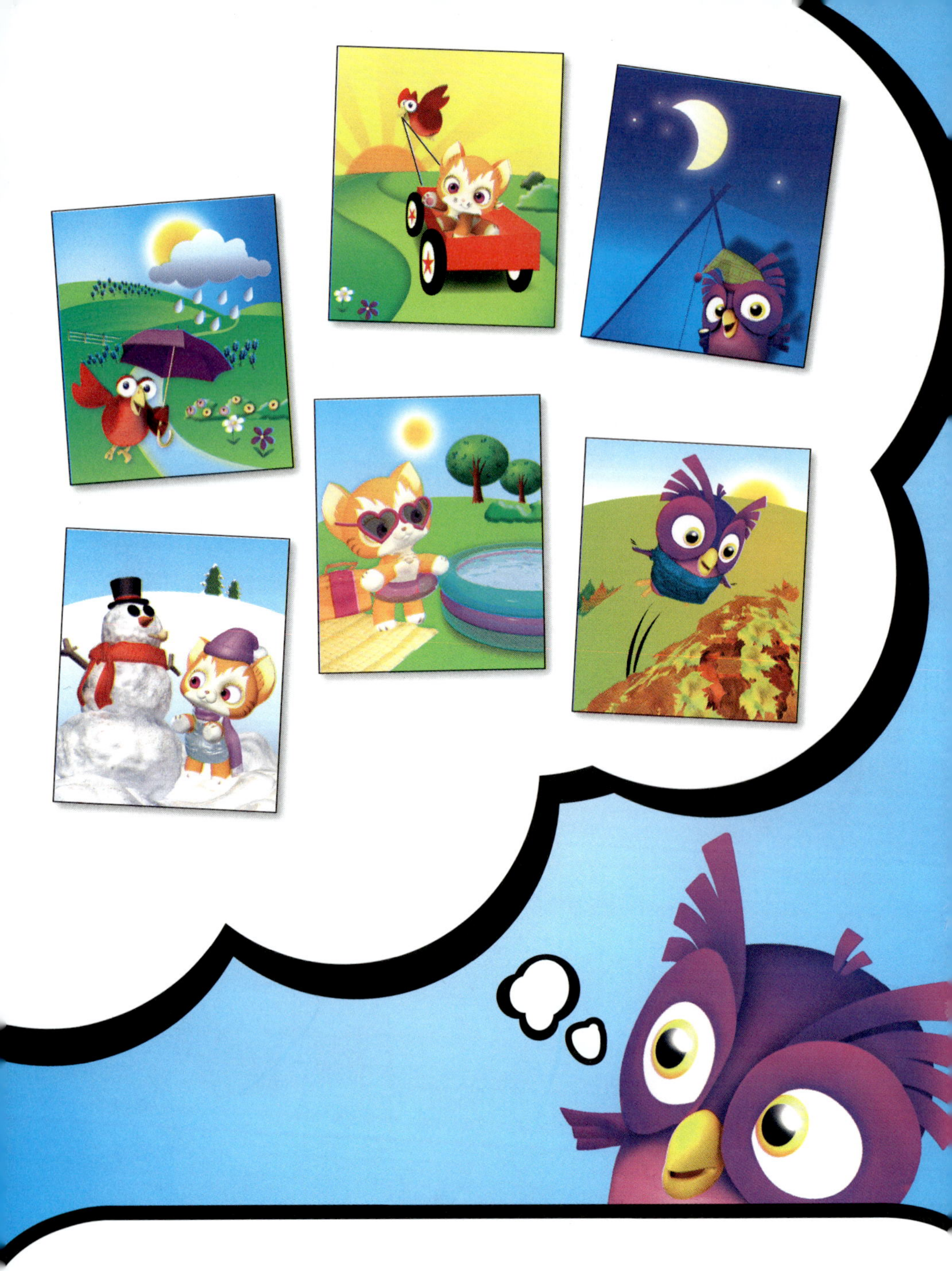

Changes!